A14404 703483

D0922837

DATE DUE

sent

T2-BTS-246

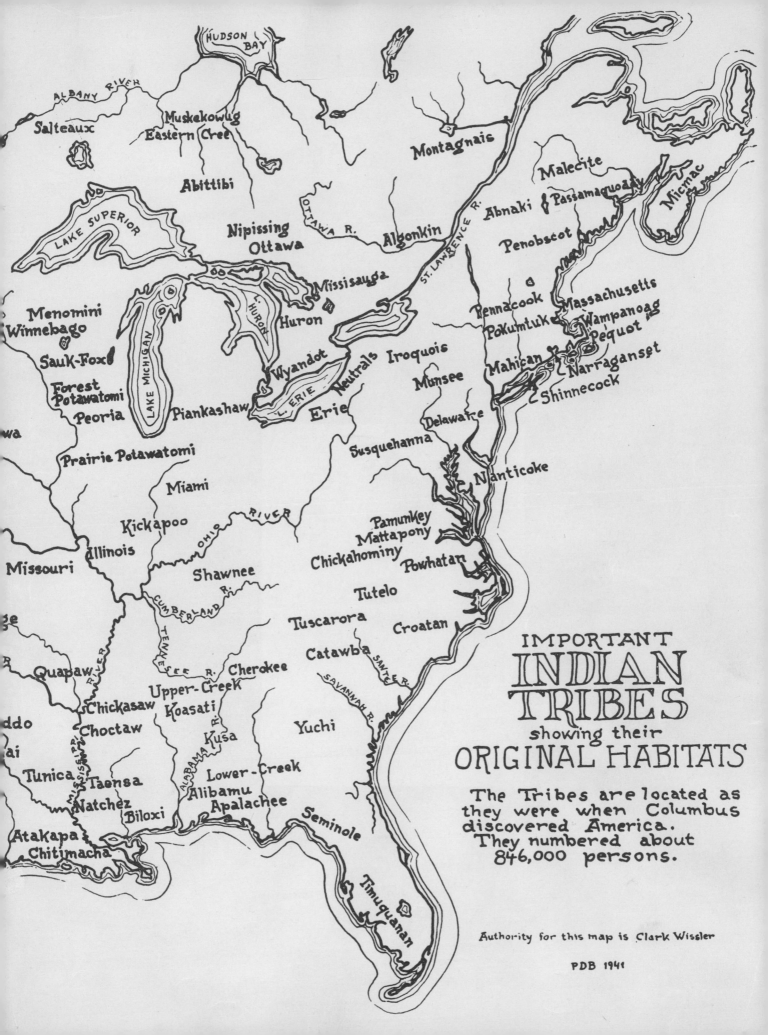

IMPORTANT
INDIAN
TRIBES
showing their
ORIGINAL HABITATS

The Tribes are located as they were when Columbus discovered America. They numbered about 846,000 persons.

Authority for this map is Clark Wissler

PDB 1941

Call No.

970.1
M178t

Accession
Number

301016
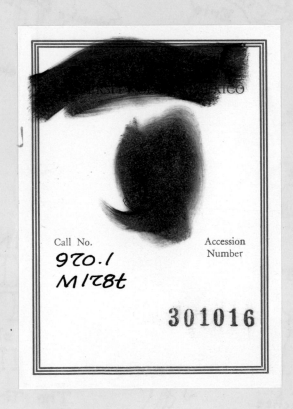

TWENTIETH CENTURY INDIANS

Navajo Woman.　　　NAVAJO RESERVATION, NEW MEXICO

TWENTIETH CENTURY

INDIANS

PHOTOGRAPHS AND TEXT BY

FRANCES COOKE MACGREGOR

WITH A FOREWORD BY CLARK WI

NEW YORK · G · P · PUTNAM'S SONS · MCMXLI

COPYRIGHT, 1941, BY FRANCES COOKE MACGREGOR

*All rights reserved. This book, or parts thereof, must
not be reproduced in any form without permission.*

Designed by Robert Josephy

MANUFACTURED IN THE UNITED STATES OF AMERICA

VAN REES PRESS · NEW YORK

UNIVERSITY OF NEW MEXICO LIBRARY

E
77
M114

To
My Father and Mother

301016

Certainly the continuance of autocratic rule, by a Federal department, over the lives of more than 200,000 citizens of this Nation is incompatible with American ideals of liberty. It also is destructive of the character and self-respect of a great race.

PRESIDENT ROOSEVELT

In urging the enactment of the Indian Reorganization Act of 1934

Foreword

WE are a proud people, reluctant to recognize that our way of life has its seamy side. So we are surprised to learn that the Indians of today regard their way of life as more desirable than our way. In spite of all our efforts to make white people of them they still hold fast to an outlook upon nature and cherish social ideals that are based upon their past and which to them appear far superior to anything we have to offer. We subjected them to terrible poverty, we racked them with threats of destruction, we took their children away from them by force, yet even this did not convince them. They died with the conviction that their spiritual and social values were worth dying for. Yet in spite of all we did to crush out the Indian's way of life he survived and is increasing in numbers. If you accept the biological law of nature that the fit survive, then the Indian is the most fit of any part of our population, since his rate of increase exceeds that of all others.

For more than half a century the Indian's resistance to our campaign of suppression has been peaceful. He has not tried to reform us. He has ignored us when he could and so gradually forced us to consider him and his influence upon our national life. To understand the situation we need most of all a realistic presentation of

ix

contemporary Indian life, not an idealized interpretative one. Clear, graphic photography can give such a record when the pictures are selected with care, as in this volume. You see the Indian at work, in everyday costume, in his home, at school, in sickness and health, in poverty and degradation. We have unintentionally made his life as hard as we could but his spirit has not been broken. It continues to express itself in his art and crafts as well as in his social ideals. We are surprised to see how quickly his feeling for art asserts itself the moment we cease to suppress it and that what emerges is his own art and not our art. His art is an expression of the spiritual values we failed to crush after several centuries of suppression.

Another worthwhile message the author has for us concerns what land means to the Indian, how intimately his spiritual values are rooted in his land. This again seems strange to us. One danger in our civilization may lie in the indifference we feel for the land which to us is just a place to lay concrete and raise up buildings. In contrast the Indian's spiritual values are rooted in the land, they are an inseparable part of it. Another point the photographs illustrate is that the Indian prefers to live out of doors. The house is chiefly a place for sleeping and resting in bad weather, for whenever possible women, men and children work outside the house. They are hardened to cold and damp but their lungs are full of good air. They feel that they are nearer to their land and to nature when out of doors. Then do not overlook the surviving types of aboriginal houses and the look of comfort that envelops them as in the photographs on pages 33, 35 and 40, in contrast to those on pages 39, 43 and 95. What has been gained by exchanging the best type of aboriginal housing for the lowest possible standard of white housing?

Then take a look at pages 97 and 99, noting that the baby-board has been tolerated in the hospital. Why not? Recent careful studies have shown that no harm results from this custom, that on the contrary Indian babies habituated to the cradle-board are quieter and more contented than those not so handled. Then remember the out-of-doors life of Indians to which this device is a satisfactory solution for the care of a baby. Why stigmatize this device as a trait of savagery? We use the Indian's foods, some of his recipes, his snow shoes, his birch bark canoes, his tobacco and pipes without feeling disgraced, so why be so intolerant of other of his devices which have merit?

At the end the author gives us a feeling of relief. She shows us that the way for the Indian will still be hard and poverty in our sense will haunt his steps for a long time, but if we give him more freedom to raise his standard of living and to cherish his spiritual and social values, he will be happier through it all and live in hope. A recent delegation of Hopi Indians to Washington said that they came not to ask charity but knowledge and wisdom as to how to protect their lands from erosion and drought. All the help they sought was expert advice as to how to solve their problem of subsistence on their land. This expresses the faith and hope of the author, it is the message she seeks to carry to the reader.

Clark Wissler

New York
April, 1941

xi

Preface

THERE are in existence today a great many vagaries and misconceptions concerning the Indians of the United States. Americans well-acquainted with Europe and Europeans or the culture of the Orient, reveal an extraordinary lack of knowledge regarding their own native population. And they express surprise at the answers to their questions on how the Indians live, what they do, what their religious beliefs are, and whether they are backward or intelligent.

Much of this is due, I think, to the fact that our school and popular books about Indians have been concerned only with Indians of the past—commonly presented in an unfavorable light—and we have been led to assume that the life of this minority group, if not definitely over, is in its last convulsive stage. Those remaining Indians, consequently, are viewed with a certain curiosity or, worse still, regarded with an arrogance born of racial prejudice and intolerance.

It was with the purpose, therefore, of attempting to clarify and correct some of these erroneous concepts and to present a true picture of Indian life as it exists today, that these photographs were taken. The written material was gathered and compiled from the writings of many scholars in the field—for which I offer grateful acknowledgment at the end of this book—as well as from my own observations while making this study. It is, of course, impossible to cover all phases of Indian life in one book or a dozen books, or to devote adequate space to all the separate tribes and no attempt is made here to do so. This is a general cross-section of contemporary Indian life offered in the hope that it may answer many of the questions which so often arise; and that it will bring into focus some of the acute problems originating from the conflict of two civilizations in which one has tried to dominate the other.

It is further hoped that by closer acquaintance with this third of a million people, who are so much a part of America and American life, a better understanding of them will be gained.

I wish to acknowledge my special indebtedness to Dr. Clark Wissler, Curator of Anthropology, American Museum of Natural History, and Mr. René d'Harnoncourt, General Manager of the Indian Arts and Crafts Board, United States Department of Interior, for reading the proofs of this book and for their constructive criticisms.

Contents

TWENTIETH CENTURY INDIANS

1. *Brief History of the Indians of the United States*

THE wave of white people which flowed from the Atlantic to the Pacific in the discovery, expansion, and settlement of America, the ever-restless movements and seekings for more fertile land, more gold, and greater forests, drove the aboriginal population of America to the poorest lands, wiped out or deprived them of their aboriginal mode and means of living, and left them to adjust themselves, in whatever way they could, to a new order of life. A once dominant race of people had become definitely and quickly a minority group. A minority to be treated with the same scorn, the same dogmatic intolerance, even the same cruelties, that some minority groups are enduring in a war-torn world today. The Indian was doomed; at least this was the intent, conscious or unconscious, of a new white world whose government fashioned laws toward this end. And doomed the Indian was, for almost four centuries. The Vanishing American—a once colorful and noble race—reduced to poverty, disease, and a state of inferiority.

Many people today are still under the impression that the Indian race is a dying one. Tourists, inspired by a new national consciousness, see a few pitiful Indians on station platforms selling cheap curios. They visit resorts where "domesticated" Indians, arrayed in buckskins and feathered bonnets, perform "old war dances" for the entertainment of the guests. And these Indians, they think, are the last representatives of a people they once read about in adventure books. It is true that at one time, and not so long ago, the Indians were on the road to extinction. But today, this is no longer true. The Indians are increasing. In fact, they have increased so rapidly in the last eight years that the birth rate among them is almost twice that of the United States white population as a whole.

It is believed by most authorities on the subject that some 10 to 25 thousand years ago those we know as Indians were a Mongoloid people who migrated in bands across Siberia, the Bering Straits, and into Alaska. From here, seeking a warmer climate, they pushed southward. Some spread across the North American continent, others went down into Central America, and still others went as far as South America. As more groups arrived, they sought new territories until almost all the habitable land was occupied.[1]

When Columbus touched the shores of the New World, there were approximately 846,000 Indians living along and between the Atlantic and Pacific coasts in what is now the United States. They were living in a state of comparative peace and contentment though raids for captives or plunder were frequent among the tribes. Now and then one tribe waged war against another but these engagements did not result in the kind of devastation

[1] See Map (front end papers).

DEPARTMENT OF THE INTERIOR

In the United States Department of the Interior is the Office of Indian Affairs, from which the administration of Indian affairs emanates. Headed by the Commissioner, the Office directs and controls through its staff and field agencies all matters pertaining to the interests of Indians.

WASHINGTON, D. C.

and destruction wrought by more advanced civilizations. On the contrary, Indian wars often amounted only to the killing of one member of an enemy tribe as a mark of warning or revenge.

They had vast amounts of fertile land, enough to provide three square miles for each individual. The tribes on the west coast had abundant hunting and fishing. Those in the center of the continent hunted wild buffalo which roamed the plains in tremendous herds. The tribes in the Southwest were mainly devoted to agriculture. On the Atlantic coast the men hunted wild deer and other animals of the forests while the women cultivated small gardens of corn. Their life was good in this land of plenty, and no man was their superior; but the darkest days they had ever known were ahead of them, for they were to be driven from place to place for years to come.

Colonizers from Europe had arrived on their shores. Men seeking religious and political freedom from their oppressors in other countries and equality with their fellow men, came over in boatloads. The Indians offered hospitality and friendship to these strange and new people from across the "big water," but it soon became apparent that the settlers intended to supplant them. They swarmed over the lands of the Indians, cut down their sheltering forests, and recklessly destroyed their source of food supply. And so the Indians rose in retaliation. They fought against the Spanish, the French, and the English; and, though their resistance was occasionally effective, in the end it was always defeat. Their villages were burned, and their women and children made innocent victims. Their bows and arrows were helpless against the steel weapons and gunpowder of the white men, and further com-

6

Local Indian administration is conducted by the U. S. Government through Indian Agencies established on the reservations. Here Government employees manage the financial, land, educational, health, police, and organizational activities of the reservation. To these offices Indians may come for help with their problems.

NAVAJO INDIAN AGENCY, WINDOW ROCK, ARIZONA

bat was futile. Submission to the whites was inevitable if they were to survive at all.

A far greater cause of death among the Indians than war were the ravages of disease brought into the country. The Indians had not been completely free of illnesses, but the prevailing diseases, in general, had not been of a fatal nature, and on the whole the race had been a comparatively healthy one. But these new diseases: smallpox, yellow fever, trachoma, and even measles—with the additional spreading of syphilis, tuberculosis, and alcoholism— raged through their villages like wildfire and swept out whole groups at a time.

As time passed and the white man's greed for more land grew, the Indians were shunted back farther and farther. Even in the far west, where the pioneers had gone in search of gold, they were pressed off their lands. All over the country where there was not actual theft of their property, there was shrewd bargaining or bribery, treaties signed under duress, the sinister implications of which the Indians could not grasp; and soon they were losing all their lands, their homes, and their means of living.

Finally in 1871, the United States Government terminated the much abused practice of treaty-making and changed to a policy based on the segregation of Indians on reservations.[2] These reservations were portions of land set aside in various sections of the country for certain groups of Indians where they could live undisturbed by further invasion. Yet even these lands set aside by promises and treaties were not to remain intact. When they

[2] Reservations had been created before 1871 but were not important until after that date.

8

seemed desirable for white use, they were carved up or whole sections taken and the Indians moved on to less fertile territory.

The result of all these destructive forces—war, disease, liquor, starvation, and loss of land—greatly diminished the Indian population. Thus in the year 1900 there were but 270,000 left, or one-quarter of the original number which were living on the land in 1492.

2. *Population, 1900-1940*

TODAY there are more than 361,000[1] Indians living in the United States. This increase in population and the current rapidity of growth are to be wondered at in the light of the treatment Indians received at the hands of the white men. What happened to bring about this great change is the question which naturally arises. How has it been possible for the Indian to survive in the face of the disastrous events which had taken place in the life of his people?

Going back to the year 1900, when there were but 270,000 survivors, the story does not suddenly change from one of persecution to one in which all wrongs are righted. On the contrary, conditions were about as hopeless as they could be and continued to remain so for a long time. Most of the Indians were then rounded up on reservations. No longer were they free to roam the countryside and hunt the wild game they needed for food, though thousands of buffalo were slaughtered for their hides by white settlers. The Indians were told to give up their tipis, wicki-ups, brush shelters, or whatever type of dwelling to which they were accustomed and to build wooden houses like the white men.

[1] U. S. Office of Indian Affairs, Jan. 1, 1940.

Navajo Woman. The majority of United States Indians are wards of the Federal Government. Indians living on reservations are free to leave them and to engage in any kind of work they desire.

NAVAJO RESERVATION, NEW MEXICO

It must be remembered here that most tribes, except those in the Southwest, had had temporary dwellings and moved from one locality to another, setting up new ones as they were needed. They were used to camp life, to the cold air that blew through their primitive homes in the night, and they were active and for the most part healthy. But these new wooden shacks with their doors and windows tightly shut were overheated and badly ventilated. Families were crowded together, and the natural result was the rapid spreading of tuberculosis and other diseases.

Food was scarce. Many were actually starving or dependent on poor rations handed out by Government agencies. Their children were torn from the family group and sent off to boarding schools established by the Government where they would learn to be like white people.

All Indian customs were frowned upon and discouraged. The men were urged to cut their hair, and they were forbidden to practice their religion, which plays such an important part in their everyday life. They were to speak English, to put aside their beadwork and weaving, cease making baskets or silver ornaments, and to become as much as possible like their conquerors. Now that the old life had been taken from them, they had nothing to do but sit and think about the past. That this could happen in a land founded on the concepts of freedom and tolerance of all men seems incredible. But happen it did; and, because these red men seemed so different, they were considered to be little more than savages and were accordingly treated as such.

It became evident as the years passed that the Indian was on the road to extinction. No people could survive under such appal-

Gayhead Indian "chief" in a powwow costume given him by a member of the Blackfeet Tribe. Not all Indians live on reservations. Some live in towns or communities as this man does.

MARTHA'S VINEYARD, MASSACHUSETTS

ling treatment. They could not throw over in a few years the habits and customs of centuries to become like white men. They could not comprehend the white man's way of living, his standards, or his desire for wealth and power. Treated with contempt, there was nothing left for them. Despair and disease became their lot.

But there were friends of the Indians. Groups of white men and women whose eyes were open to their plight were agitating for a reform in the administration of Indian affairs. A few men in Government circles, including President Hoover, saw the need for action. They felt that something had to be done to restore to these people some part of the life that had been taken from them and to erase, if possible, the blot on our national honor made by hundreds of broken promises and treaties.

Consequently, in 1928, when sufficient pressure had been brought to bear, a governmental investigation into the state of Indian affairs was conducted and groundwork laid for a new Government policy. These new plans to return to the Indians some of their lost rights and privileges, to give them tribal self-government, and to prevent further loss of land were the aims of what is now known as the Indian Reorganization Act passed by Congress in 1934. John Collier, who had worked for and with the Indians for many years, was made Commissioner of the Office of Indian Affairs in the Department of the Interior. Under his zestful guidance, along with the co-operation of other private groups, a new day for the Indian dawned.

As concerted efforts were made to give medical aid to the Indians, to alter the evils of the educational policies and to make

Pomo Indian who is head of the tribal council which governs the affairs of his community. Indians can vote and hold land. They are also entitled to the same protection the Constitution offers other U. S. citizens.

MANCHESTER, CALIFORNIA

some land restoration, their lives began to take on a new meaning. As a culminating result, their numbers have increased to 351,000 and their race is no longer a dying one. It must not be assumed from this increase that all is well with the Indians and that they are now a completely contented people. This is far from true. Though their standards of living have been raised somewhat, there still remains the fact that most of them are living on the fringe of poverty and even beneath it.

It is important to know that this one-third of a million native Americans are not all alike and, according to the different tribes to which they belong, they vary in customs, beliefs, and modes of living. They also differ considerably in physical appearance, temperament, and mentality just as people of other nations do. There is no standard Indian type as popularized by fiction or the Indian on the nickel. It is true that some possess the same high cheekbones, straight nose, and thin lips (for example the Sioux), but many Indians have round faces, broad noses, and full lips (for example the Shoshoni). While some have very dark skin and black hair, others have light skin and brownish hair. Nor are the Indians as tall as we picture them, the average height of the Indian being less than that of the white man.

About 241,000 live on reservations, most of which are west of the Mississippi River. Arizona, New Mexico, and Oklahoma contain nearly one-half of the entire Indian population though large groups of them live in California, Montana, South Dakota, Wisconsin, and Washington. On the eastern side of the Mississippi there are about 63,000. In fact, all but a few states have some Indians living in them. In those states having no large reservations,

A Papago Indian who is driver of the school bus for Indian children. All Indians born in the United States are citizens of this country. All Federal Offices are open to Indians and, with the exception of a few States, all State offices.

PAPAGO RESERVATION, ARIZONA

there may be found tribes ranging anywhere from a hundred to a thousand in number.[2]

There are approximately 300 different tribes in the country today and about 250 different languages and dialects are still spoken.[3] For example, there are the Navajo, the Pima, Papago, Pueblo, and Apache tribes living in the Southwest. In the Pacific states are the Pomo, Paiute, Yakima, and Klamath tribes. In the Plains area are the Sioux, Arapaho, Cheyenne, and Kiowa, and on the Eastern coast live the Passamaquoddy, Narragansett, and Seminole. These are a few of the tribes in existence today; and, as they speak different languages, English is becoming the common one of communication. In the Southwest, Spanish is used to some extent.

All Indians are not full-bloods for over a long period of time there has been much intermarriage with the whites. Today almost one-half of them are an admixture. In the Southwest, however, where contact with whites has not been so marked, the Indians have remained for the most part full-blood. The number of full-bloods in this particular section amounts to 97.6 per cent of their total population.

Whether the Indian population will increase in Indian blood or white blood, time alone will reveal. At present it is believed by some that the limitations of reservation life will be a restraining factor in intermarriage with whites, with a consequent increase in pure Indian stock.

[2] See Map (rear end papers).
[3] Clark Wissler, *Indians of the United States* (New York: Doubleday, Doran & Co., 1940).

Pima

Yuma

Navajo

Maricopa

Hopi

Apache

TRIBAL TYPES

Full-blood Papago

¾ Pomo—¼ white

½ Pomo—½ white

1/16 Pomo—15/16 white

Full-blood Pueblo

Full-blood Arapaho

FULL-BLOODS AND MIXED-BLOODS

3. *Land – Major Indian Problem Today*

THE life of the Indian has for centuries been bound to the land. His ancient belief was that the earth was a mother who provided food for her children. The lands of the earth were free, and the abundant streams and hunting grounds were for all men. These things, necessary to the existence of the race, were not to be appropriated by any one group or individual.

It was found in time that the spontaneous production of the soil could be augmented by the planting of seeds for better crops but this required the presence of the planter on the land he cultivated. This occupancy was the only land tenure recognized by the Indians, a privilege abruptly terminated if the land was not cultivated and allowed to go to waste.

The Indians have found it difficult, therefore, to understand the accumulation of hundreds or thousands of acres by an individual white man which are allowed to lie idle or are destroyed by reckless farming and lumbering. For Indians had great respect for the land. They recognized its value not in terms of profits as do white men, but as something to be regarded with

21

a kind of reverence. Today, the majority of Indians continue to feel this way toward land. It is part of their life and such tremendous losses as they have endured have made their life a hard one.

By the year 1887, the white men had taken from them all the land in the United States but 138,000,000 acres; and, as the years passed, even this amount was reduced. Tribal lands within reservations were now divided among the individual members, and the surplus land declared open to white settlers. By 1933, Indian holdings had dwindled to around 48,000,000 acres, or approximately $2\frac{1}{2}\%$ of their original holdings. Almost two-thirds of the Indians were now landless or had land too poor in quality to provide them with a living. By 1939, 2,780,000 acres were restored to them by the Government, a small amount considering that which had been taken from them.

Most of that remaining in Indian ownership today is exceedingly poor and unproductive. Much of it is desert and mountainous. Limited in amount to small, widely scattered areas, this land has been vastly overgrazed by livestock. Soil that should never have been broken has been plowed. The overgrazing of land, particularly in the Southwest region, and the reckless timber-cutting in other sections has caused rapid erosion. The top soil has washed away, and great arroyos have spread out over the plains. On the Papago Reservation in southern Arizona are miles of arid stretches washed clean of every blade of grass. Heavy rains have left dry sandy gulches, and here in one small district alone 105 cattle died of starvation in one year. On the Navajo Reservation, which is as large as Connecticut, Massachusetts, Rhode Is-

Erosion. Overgrazing and heavy rains have resulted in miles of scarred, barren land on this reservation. There are 174 Indian reservations in the United States.

PAPAGO RESERVATION, ARIZONA

land, and New Jersey combined, a tremendous part of the land is semidesert, and water is scarce. In the Pueblo of Acoma, New Mexico, where Indians have had their homes for centuries, they were recently faced with a desperate situation. Thousands of sheep roamed aimlessly over a range too poor to sustain them. The growth of vegetation was so sparse that in a short time it would have vanished completely and so too would the sheep. Government experts forestalled a potential disaster for the Indians by suggesting that the number of sheep be reduced to the carrying capacity of the land. The remaining stock, therefore, would not only have enough to eat but would not destroy all the vegetation.

In California, a recent report of the Resettlement Administration revealed that of the land on 132 small reservations and rancherias, only 5% of the total amount is of any value for agriculture, grazing, or timber. The balance, for the most part, consists of brush-covered hills, rugged mountains, and desert regions. In a state noted for its rich soil and tremendous amounts of farm produce, it is obvious that the Indians have received the worst pieces of land in this particular instance. They are, as a result, enduring great privation, and many have had to be placed on relief rolls in order to keep them and their families from starvation.

Many governmental departments, in an effort to aid the Indians, are engaged in programs to help them with the land they have. Rivers and streams have been dammed to create reservoirs of water for the irrigation of dry lands. The kinds of crops best suited to the soil are planted to provide food for livestock or food for hungry Indians. They are being taught to preserve their forests by replanting trees where others have been cut down. The Soil-

Drought. One of 105 cattle which died of starvation in one year in the Chuck-ut-kuk district on the Papago Reservation. There are eleven districts on this reservation.

PAPAGO RESERVATION, ARIZONA

Conservation Department is helping them to preserve the land they have by the prevention of further disastrous erosion caused by floods, rains, and winds.

In spite of this assistance, however, the major Indian problem today continues to be that of land. The survival of the Indian depends not only on the holding of that which he has, but also on the acquisition of more. This additional land must be of superior quality to that he now owns if he is to become entirely self-supporting.

Irrigation. Desert land in Nevada, where only sagebrush grew, is being irrigated by water brought in from a distant river by the U.S. Government. The Office of Indian Affairs in the Department of Interior is in charge of all reservations.

FALLON, NEVADA

The Pima Indians in Northern Arizona have better land than most
Indians. Here a Pima plows his land for spring planting.

SALT RIVER INDIAN RESERVATION, ARIZONA

4. *Indian Housing*

A MENTAL picture of tipis and wigwams is formed in the minds of most people when they think of Indian habitations. But these were by no means the only types of Indian houses. Contrary to popular opinion, Indians have lived and do live in many different kinds of dwellings which vary considerably in form and construction.

The difference in the type of shelter is determined by the physiography of occupied areas, the kind of climate with which the Indians must contend, and the available materials at hand for building. It depends, too, to what degree the Indian has been influenced by the white man. Where the impact of white civilization has been marked, the Indians have adopted the white man's type of shelter. We find also that certain tribes retain their own peculiar type of house that was originally adopted for a particular need. A recent survey of Indian homes showed that 54,729 families live in permanent dwellings and 9,485 live in brush shelters, hogans, wigwams, or other temporary dwellings.

In the Southwest, where the Pueblo Indians live, the scarcity of wood in that section led the Indians to build their houses of blocks of sandstone or adobe. Originally they were constructed in terrace fashion, one house on top of the other, the roof of one forming a sort of front yard for the house above it. In each unit lived a family, and on the outside of each, wooden ladders led from one roof to another. These massive and compact settlements were the first apartment houses of America and were called "pueblos" by the Spanish, meaning village. They were erected in this manner to serve as a defense against invading tribes. Many of them remain in use today though the present tendency is to build individual houses which are rectangular in shape. The adobe homes of the pueblos are probably the most practical in modern times of any tribe. They are sturdy in construction and suitable for the arid climate, being cool in summer and warm in winter. The women usually own the homes and, though the men assist with the hauling and placing of heavy beams, build the houses themselves. One may often see an Indian woman plastering the walls of her home when it is in need of repair. The rooms of the houses are small, and the hard floors are of pounded earth or adobe and are usually well swept. Windows and a corner fireplace with a chimney have been introduced in the newer houses.

Papago and Pima Indians, the desert dwellers of southern Arizona, likewise build their homes of adobe. These are rectangular in shape and the roofs are usually thatched. The Papagos utilize ribs or poles made from the cactus, ocotillo, or creosote plants for the sides of the house, and fill in the spaces with adobe, while the Pimas on the other hand plaster adobe over a framework of boards. Both tribes, however, often construct their houses entirely of adobe brick.

In the northern part of Arizona and New Mexico live the semi-

Cliff dwellings were prehistoric houses built in the faces of cliffs or canyon walls as a defense against invading tribes. Inhabited by the ancestors of the modern Pueblo Indians as far back as the tenth century, most of them, like this one, are in ruins today.

PUYÉ RUINS, NEW MEXICO

nomadic Navajo people. Here may be found a very distinctive type of dwelling: the hogan, of which there are eight different kinds. These are all fairly simple in structure, being conical or dome-shaped and rather low. A smoke hole [1] is in the roof of each, and the blanket or wooden door always faces east. [2] Only one day is necessary for the building of a hogan, for friends come to aid in its construction. Piñon logs, cedar bark and boughs are gathered near by and placed in position. A generous supply of damp earth is employed for the roofing, and mud is packed in the cracks between the logs. The more modern hogans are hexagonal, and the walls are somewhat straighter and higher. The floors are dirt, and sheepskins are used to sit or sleep on. During the winter, a fire is kept burning in the center for warmth and for cooking. When the weather becomes warm, the Navajo family moves into a summer house. This is commonly a primitive structure of four posts supporting a roof of pine boughs and earth, which provides protection from the hot sun.

Had we visited the Great Plains region in the early days, we would have found such tribes as the Sioux, Arapaho, Comanche, and Kiowa living in tipis. These were made of a circular framework of poles brought together near the top and covered with buffalo hides. Because these Indians moved over the Plains hunting the bison, they needed a portable shelter which could be easily transported, first by dogs and later by horses. Today few tipis are in use; and, where it is still necessary to move about, the modern Indian uses a tent he has bought in a store, and this he carries in his wagon or car from one camping place to another.

[1] To allow the evil spirits to escape.
[2] It is believed that the gods assemble here at dawn.

32

Indian apartment house occupied by the Pueblo Indians at Taos, New Mexico.

The Kickapoo Indians in Oklahoma live in small communities, and their winter houses are most picturesque and unusual. These are oval-shaped lodges or wigwams made of branches tied together forming a framework. Flag reeds gathered from the river beds are woven into mats by the women and placed over the frame until it is completely covered. On top of the roof large pieces of bark are laid for additional protection. Such houses are sufficiently sealed against heavy rains and cold, except perhaps for the square hole in the center of the roof from which the smoke escapes. The door is nothing more than heavy blankets or old quilts, and inside this one-room house a fire is set in the center of a dirt floor. Grass mats cover a slightly raised circular platform in the room where the family sleeps at night. The Kickapoo also have a summer house constructed of branches and bark. This is rectangular with a gabled roof. A raised shelf or bunk is built inside for sleeping, and the cool night air blows through the open sides.

In California and Nevada the Indians are scattered about on small reservations and rancherias. Over an extended period of time they have been in close contact with white men and, as a result, have adopted their frame houses. Since most of these Indians belong to that economic group known as the "ill-housed," the majority of dwellings are squalid one-room shacks built of inferior material and totally inadequate for decent living. Father, mother, children, grandparents, and often long-visiting relatives can be found sharing a couple of beds or blankets on the floor. Dogs and children play on the dusty floor boards, and disease spreads rapidly under the prevailing conditions.

Still another type of habitation may be found among the

Papago house. In the desert where they live, Papagos build their homes of adobe and the stalks of desert plants. This house is made of adobe bricks, and the ribs of the Ocotillo bush.

PAPAGO RESERVATION, ARIZONA

Apaches of New Mexico, Arizona, and Oklahoma. Known as wickiups, they are crude brush, dome-shaped lodges, covered whenever possible with pieces of canvas. At one time such primitive dwellings were adequate, for the Apaches moved about the countryside raiding other tribes, and they used them only for temporary purposes. Today, with the Indians living in permanent communities, these habitations with their accumulation of dirt are little better than disease-ridden hovels. Under the encouragement of Government agencies, however, some Apache tribes are now adopting more substantial frame houses.

The Cherokee Indians, living in the woodland section of Eastern Oklahoma, have log cabins. A few members of this tribe, as well as some of the neighboring Osage Indians, have been made wealthy by the discovery of oil and have acquired elaborate homes similar to those of the more affluent white people. However, these are very exceptional cases. More often in the United States are to be found Indians who, having lost their land, have moved to the outskirts of a town in order to be near a Government agency where they may obtain relief money or rations necessary for their sustenance. Their homes are mere shanties put together with old pieces of lumber and corrugated tin and usually situated near the town dumping grounds.

Not all Indian homes are poor, and many have comfortable well-kept quarters, but Indian housing on the whole may be said to be definitely below the standards required for healthful living. The United States Office of Indian Affairs is cognizant of the existing conditions and knows that it is impossible for any people to work well or to maintain their self-respect when forced to live

Navajo house. A modern and well-built hogan in which this family lives. These newer hexagonal hogans are made of closely fitted logs and an earth-covered roof. Where timber is available, these structures are replacing the older type houses.

NAVAJO RESERVATION, NEW MEXICO

under such difficulties. There is a great need for the rehabilitation of the Indian, and one of the first steps toward accomplishing this is the improvement of his living quarters. With the aid of an emergency fund the Bureau has been able to erect houses for a few of the hopelessly destitute. In South Dakota the Office of Indian Affairs established on fertile land, housing facilities which included house, toilet, and poultry house for a number of separate families. The immediate result was improvement in their morale and a renewed diligence toward their work. As Indian housing is improved, so too will be their lives.

Store tents have supplanted most of the skin tipis once used by the Plains Indians. These tents with stoves and radios belong to some Arapaho families who will move to a new camping spot in the spring.

CHEYENNE RESERVATION, OKLAHOMA

Kickapoo winter house. Woven mats of flag reeds keep this house warm and waterproof. A wooden mortar and pestle for grinding corn can be seen at the left.

SHAWNEE RESERVATION, OKLAHOMA

Kickapoo winter house under construction. Saplings are placed in position and lashed securely to form a framework. Mats will be added to cover the frame.

SHAWNEE RESERVATION, OKLAHOMA

*Kickapoo summer house. The rear section with the latticed roof is
used for the sleeping quarters. The front of the house provides
shade and protection from summer rains. Here the women work
during the day and prepare the meals.*

SHAWNEE RESERVATION, OKLAHOMA

California Indians have adopted the frame houses of the white men. Many of their homes like those of poor rural whites are one-room shacks built of inferior materials.

PINOLEVILLE, CALIFORNIA

Apache wickiup. Originally used for temporary shelters when Apaches moved about the countryside during raids. Undesirable for permanent living, they are nevertheless used today by many Apaches, who prefer them to other types of houses.

FORT MCDOWELL, ARIZONA

5. *Subsistence*

THE old way of living has passed for most Indians, and they have had to adjust themselves to a new kind of civilization in America, developed by white men. A new order has been established in which business, property, and money are the foundations of American economic life. The pressure of this system has forced the Indians to adapt themselves to it as well as they can, for the land is no longer theirs to rove at will, hunting wild game for food and clothing when their supplies run low. Instead, they must go to a store and buy part of their food. They must have clothes to wear, and trucks and tools with which to work, and above all they must have money to purchase these articles. In order to exist, therefore, the Indians of today have turned to various kinds of labor activities. As a people whose life was lived in the out-of-doors, it is natural that they should, on the whole, follow out-of-door occupations.

Sheep raising is engaged in by many individual Indians, but the tribe whose main source of income is derived from sheep is the Navajo. Navajos have raised sheep for at least a hundred years, but loss of land caused by erosion, and lack of vegetation have made this business today less profitable and one of many problems.

Many young married Indians who have been to school find it increasingly difficult to support themselves and their children on a small flock of sheep. Discouraged, they go to the neighboring towns to obtain jobs as mechanics or domestic workers. In time, however, the majority of them usually return to the reservation, preferring to live as their own people do, even though their flocks are small. The wool and sheep are exchanged with a Government-licensed trader for necessary groceries and dry goods or sold to commercial buyers. The income for the average Navajo family which includes about seven members is small. Measured in goods and cash, it is about $500 a year.

Cattle raising is a more important Indian occupation. In 1937, 21,287 Indians owned cattle. In South Dakota the Sioux, who are expert horsemen and who once rode the range in pursuit of the buffalo, have taken naturally to cattle raising. They love the life of the cowboy, the colorful dress, and the hard riding it requires. In Montana, the Blackfeet and northern Cheyenne Indians live by means of cattle raising as do the Apache and Papago in Arizona. With the help of Government stockmen the Indians are learning to raise better stock and to use scientific methods in the care of them.

In pre-Columbian days farming was the most important occupation of the village tribes in New Mexico and Arizona. For centuries these Pueblo Indians, who had built their homes for stability and permanence, have been tilling farms and irrigating them by man-made ditches. Corn, squash, and beans, which they grew hundreds of years ago, are still their main crops today though such European foods as wheat are now grown. In other tribes where

46

A Papago rides the range in search of stray cattle.

PAPAGO RESERVATION, ARIZONA

hunting was more important, the cultivation of gardens was considered woman's work. Today, however, Indian men have been forced to take up agriculture in order to support themselves, and they have had to learn to grow the white man's crops and to use his tools. Those who have had good land and a means of irrigation have become able farmers. Many of these former hunters like the Sioux and Shoshoni are advancing rapidly in the raising of crops. And in Oregon, Washington, and Idaho as well, Indians who once lived primarily by fishing are now engaged in farming.

In California and Nevada, where Indians have so little land to cultivate, practically all of them have been forced to work for wages. Seasonal employment by white men is now their main source of income. This work includes the picking of fruit, hops, cotton, and other crops. As they ripen at different times, whole families move from ranch to ranch, the women and children laboring beside the men. Some livestock work is afforded them as well as a small amount of lumbering in the northern part of the state. During these seasons of employment enough money is usually earned to answer their needs for the time being and, if used sparingly, can be extended for the purchase of supplies for the long winter ahead. In recent years, however, a tremendous influx of migrant workers from the Middle West, reduced to a state where work at any wage is a godsend, have swarmed over the agricultural centers of California. These people have added greatly to the already precarious position of the Indians. Available work has been diminished by too many anxious hands, and the consequent decrease in wages has, in turn, left the Indians worse off than ever. There is little opportunity for work in the winter

48

Paiute and Shoshoni Indians dip their cattle in a disinfecting bath to remove harmful ticks. Such scientific care of cattle has been taught the Indians by government experts.

FALLON, NEVADA

months, and so the Indians must depend on what they have saved and what the streams and forests can provide. Near the coast they catch and smoke salmon, and in the central section acorns are gathered and stored for winter food. This helps to sustain them but it is only a weak prop in their frail economic foundation.

The balance of their income is derived from relief work. This is offered by the W.P.A. and other relief projects, and direct relief from the Federal Government and private sources. A report on "Human Dependency and Economic Survey of the Sacramento Indian Jurisdiction in California," gives the result of a survey made of 2,649 Indians, which discloses the following startling facts: The wages earned by seasonal employment amounted to 80.4% of their income, the income derived from their own livestock and agriculture amounted to 6.5%, and miscellaneous moneys, primarily relief, added up to 13.1%. The total income in cash was $374,472.06 or $141.36 per person per year.

There are hundreds of Indians who have no farms, livestock, or even jobs with white men, and consequently no means of support. Some of these have been employed in recent years in the Indian division of the Civilian Conservation Corps. During 1938, some 6,000 Indian men worked on Indian lands to improve them. Fencing, reseeding, the building of roads, firetrails and firebreaks, the elimination of pests, and the checking of erosion are some of the projects carried on under Government supervision.

A few tribes have organized co-operative industries in which the families who give their services receive part of the profits. In Alaska a salmon cannery has been built, in Washington a project for the culture of oysters has started, and in Nevada some tribal

In California the greater part of wages is obtained from seasonal employment by white men. This Pomo Indian is pruning pear trees and later on may be hired to pick hops or grapes.

UKIAH, CALIFORNIA

land owned by the Paiute and Shoshoni Indians is being cultivated for badly needed hay.

But Indian men alone are not the only ones who contribute to the support of their families. Indian women, besides taking care of their homes and children, do much to augment the family income. Navajo women sit busily before their looms weaving wool into attractive blankets to be exchanged at the trading post for clothes, groceries, or cash. Pueblo women earn money by making pottery to sell to tourists. Baskets are woven by Pomo, Hopi, Apache, Papago, and Pima women, and beaded moccasins and trinkets are made by Arapaho, Kiowa, and Zuni women for the tourist trade.

In order fully to understand the Indians in connection with the prevailing economic pattern in the United States, their own concepts must be appreciated. They lack almost completely any comprehension of the competition necessary for living in the white man's world. They have never understood the accumulation and the hoarding of wealth by white men, for to them a man was not rich by what he possessed but by what he gave away. When times were good for the Indians, everyone had plenty to eat. When times were hard, no Indian withheld his own possessions when others were in need. A man who gave away the most, therefore, was considered the richest man. Consequently, the making of money and the saving of it for "a rainy day" does not mean very much to the majority of Indians. They regard the white man who sacrifices his health and leisure in order to acquire a fortune as very strange indeed. Which of these philosophies is superior is debatable, but the fact remains that the retention of such attitudes

"As straight as an arrow" these Washo Indians furrow the land on a white man's ranch. Driving their horses from one white marker to another (seen in background) their keenness of eye makes them preferable to white men for such work.

MINDEN, NEVADA

by the Indians has led to discouragement and frustration among them. Finding their traditional concepts impossible in the white economic structure, has caused, in many instances, feelings of antagonism toward the whites and toward the Government. But, living in a white man's world, the Indian has, perforce, come to realize that money is an important requisite for subsistence. All he asks, however, is the opportunity to earn enough to provide the necessities of life for himself and his family. Such opportunities, it appears, are limited. A survey of Indian incomes in 131 jurisdictions showed that, outside of four wealthy jurisdictions, the average Indian received $161 a year.

In a country endowed by nature with an abundance of resources, where the riches of the earth have been so bountiful that they have forced the white man of the present generation to dump his potatoes into the rivers, to destroy his surplus orange crops, to leave his figs and prunes and peaches rotting on the ground where they have fallen, to pay men for not raising tobacco, for plowing up his land, and for working less—a paradox does indeed exist.

Clamming is one of the occupations of the Wampanoag Indians of Gayhead on Martha's Vineyard, Massachusetts. This small community of about 160 inhabitants—one of the few Indian settlements left on the Eastern Seaboard—supports itself mainly by fishing, cultivation of cranberries, and pottery making.

Coastal Indians in Northern California who have access to rivers running through their lands, still spear and net salmon. A Pomo Indian has stocked his smokehouse with fish for his winter food supply, when employment is difficult to obtain.

MANCHESTER, CALIFORNIA

An Apache woman weaves a basket which she hopes to sell at an Indian trading post or to tourists. The dress she wears is the tribal costume of Apache women and is called by them a "camp dress." These were originally copied from the dresses worn by the wives of early missionaries and army officers.

FORT McDOWELL, ARIZONA

*To earn money a Papago drives his wagon into the hills to gather
wood. Later he will haul it seventy miles to Tucson, where he will
sell it to white men.*

PAPAGO RESERVATION, ARIZONA

Pueblo women make pottery to sell to tourists. Here a group of them are about to display their wares to prospective buyers. (Notice the buckskin moccasins on two of the women.)

SANTA CLARA PUEBLO, NEW MEXICO

*With the average Indian income only $160 a year, some Indians
must turn to their agencies for relief. These few Pima Indians, who
have no means of support, wait in line at the Pima Indian Agency
for their weekly supply of food rations.*

SALT RIVER RESERVATION, ARIZONA

6. *Surviving Native Culture*

AGAINST the inroads of modern civilization, modern economy, and modern social concepts upon the aboriginal life in America, there are still in evidence today many manifestations of a surviving culture to which the Indian has tenaciously clung. In the face of such powerful forces as those imposed on him by the white men, it has been a dramatic and romantic struggle for the Indian to retain a vestige of the habits and customs of his ancestors. At this point we may ask why the Indian insists on clinging to his primitive methods when our age of streamlined trains, frozen foods, and advanced scientific methods has so much to offer. It should not be so, but it is, nevertheless, necessary that we remind ourselves that other people have a heritage of beliefs and customs which means as much to them as ours does to us. We have become so accustomed to thinking that our way of living is superior, we assume that anyone who does not do as we do must either be very shiftless or exceedingly stupid. The Indian, however, has not found the white man's way superior to his in all respects, and until such time as he does he will in all probability continue along those same paths he has followed for so many generations.

The apogee of Indian culture was reached thousands of years ago under the Mayas of Mexico. The high development of the arts and sciences demonstrated without doubt the intelligence and ability of the Indians to achieve one of the most brilliant civilizations known to early man. Such heights were never attained by the Indians north of the Rio Grande, but before the arrival of the white man they had developed a textile art, agriculture, religions, complex political organizations, and diversified societies.

With the appearance of the invaders came many changes and innovations in Indian ways and customs; and the economic and material side of their culture was significantly affected. Many of the white man's things were desirable and convenient, such as horses, clothes, knives, and liquor. Money became a necessity for participation in this economic pattern. Under the existing order, with innumerable problems and adjustments to be met, some tribes found the pressure too great, and lost their identity as such. Some members died off while others drifted into neighboring tribes. What degree of civilization had been reached in many instances, was abruptly terminated by a more powerful one now dominating them. One consequence of this disruption is aptly described in the writings of Dr. Alfred Kidder, noted anthropologist. "In the 16th century the Pueblos had fallen from many of their old ranges, were reduced in numbers and had lost some of their former skill in material accomplishments, but their customs had not been changed and they still held out undismayed among their savage enemies. There can be little doubt that had they been allowed to work out their own salvation, they would have eventually overcome their

Indians live out of doors as much as possible. Sewing machine and stove have been moved outside by this Pima family, who use their house during good weather for sleeping only.

SALT RIVER RESERVATION, ARIZONA

difficulties, and might well have built up a civilization of a sort not yet attempted by any group of men. It is the tragedy of native American history that so much human effort has come to naught and that so many hopeful experiments in life and living were cut short by the devastating blight of the white man's arrival."

But in spite of the pressure of a new civilization, a marked degree of resistance remains in evidence. Though much of his ancient culture has passed, the Indian still retains today those fundamental values which play an important part in his existence. He has clung, with varying degrees of intensity, to his communal life and social organizations, in spite of relentless attempts to obliterate them. In his religion and tribal rites particularly is the survival of his culture manifest, and he retains many of his everyday customs in the face of "the modern way." His philosophy, which has given him the ability to stand fast, his great dignity in the face of adversity, and the innate faith in his race, are still qualities essentially his own.

If we visited all the Indian reservations and communities in the United States, we would find numerous concrete examples of this tendency to cling to "the old way." We would also find as we moved from one section of the country to another that modes of living, houses, dress, manners, habits, games, occupations, and religious beliefs differ to a surprising degree. This is because in early times, groups of Indians, spread as they were over a vast territory, developed their own distinct culture patterns, or modes of living. Where their customs are similar, and for the purpose of classification, they have been grouped by scientists into areas known as the

An old Yuma woman, like most Indian women, does her mending while sitting out of doors in the sun. The contraption at her back is a doghouse.

ARIZONA

Plains, Plateau, California, North Pacific Coast, Eastern Woodland, Southeastern and Southwestern Areas.[1]

We would notice, first of all, that Indians continue to carry on most of their activities out-of-doors. They are a people whose life has been closely attuned to nature, and even when they live in a white man's house they prefer to cook, sew, wash clothes, and live as much as possible under the sky rather than under a roof.

We would not see Indians wearing buckskin clothes and feathered war bonnets, except perhaps at a pageant or fair staged for tourists who expect Indians to wear them. But we would observe that while most Indians now wear American clothes many tribes retain some part of the costume worn in early days. For example, in Taos, one of the oldest pueblos in New Mexico, the men wear their hair in two braids, and the women cut their hair to form bangs down to the eyebrows. All of them wear cotton blankets that cover their heads, and the men wear a second blanket wrapped about the hips. The men once wore buckskin leggings, but today, due to the scarcity of deer skins, a man may wear American trousers so long as he cuts the seat out of them. This somehow makes them resemble leggings and is acceptable.

Navajo men have adopted store shirts and trousers, but they continue to wear moccasins and a colored band around their heads. Most of the older men keep their hair long and knotted in the back. The women are more colorful, for their costume consists of a full-flowing calico skirt and a bright-colored velveteen tunic.

[1] Clark Wissler, *The American Indian* (3rd ed.; New York: Oxford University Press, 1938).

Indian women prefer to work out of doors. This Pomo woman boils her clothes in a tin can and pounds them with a stick.

PINOLEVILLE, CALIFORNIA

Earrings, necklaces, and bracelets of silver and turquoise or shell are worn as ornaments.

The Seminole Indians of Florida have retained the greater part of their original tribal costume. The women wear long full skirts and a blouse of bright colors in many designs. Strands of beads adorn their arms, and around the neck they are worn in such numbers that they form a stiff collar from their shoulders to their chins. The headdress is a turban of cloth from which emerge feathered plumes. The men, although dressing in regular trousers and hats, continue to wear the colored, loose blouse of more ancient times.

In many Indian settlements food is prepared as it was in the early days. In California, acorns, formerly a substantial part of Indian diet, are still regarded as an important food. These are gathered by the women and children and stored in miniature brush tipis. When needed, the acorns are removed from the tipis and ground in stone holes or mortars with a stone pestle. Hot water is poured through the meal to remove the bitter tannin. Placed in a basket, in which hot rocks have been added to heat the water, the meal is boiled until it becomes a palatable acorn mush.

In pueblo villages in the Southwest, the women grind their corn on the grinding stones and bake their bread in the mud ovens outside their homes.

To store grain the Pima Indians employ large storage baskets made of straw, twigs, and adobe. Sometimes an Indian may have two or three of these baskets in his yard. These are not only examples of Indian inventiveness but are excellent for keeping the dampness from the grain.

68

On the Pacific Coast acorns, once a substantial part of native diet, are still gathered to provide a reserve food supply. Stored in brush tipis placed on wooden platforms, they are available during the winter months, when other foods are scarce.

FRESNO COUNTY, CALIFORNIA

The drying of deer meat, beef, or fish to preserve it for future use is a custom which continues. Some Indians hang their meat from a tree to dry and allow the smoke from a slow-burning fire to protect it from flies. Other Indians build smokehouses in which the meat is smoked for days until ready for storing.

Wampum or Indian money is, of course, no longer a medium of exchange, but the shell beads which were used for wampum are still made for ornamental purposes. The Pomo Indians use large clam shells that are broken up and ground on sandstone until the pieces are nearly round. After a hole has been drilled in these, the shells are polished on a slab of stone and then strung for wearing.

If we visited the Apaches in Arizona, we would observe many of the people wearing tattoo marks on their foreheads, chest, and arms. It is said that long ago, when they were a warring and raiding people, the Apaches found it necessary to mark their babies in case they were captured by other tribes. If this happened, the children might eventually be recovered by means of their identification mark.[2] These days have passed, but the custom of tattooing has continued, and today many men and women may be found wearing these bluish markings. However, the absence of tattooing on the very young members of the tribe would seem to indicate that this practice is passing.

A strong factor of past Indian life was blood relationship. To-day to a slightly lesser degree it continues to be the foundation of their unity. It is on the basis of this consanguinity that one

[2] This is one explanation of Apache tattooing. Other explanations are offered, but it has not been possible to ascertain which of these is authentic.

70

*An old Mono Indian woman winnows her acorns in preparation
for making acorn meal.*

FRESNO COUNTY, CALIFORNIA

family calls upon another in time of need, and that sharing with one another is a customary feature of their everyday life. Where the economic and civil order of the whites has been strongly felt, however, and the need for protection from outsiders, which once demanded a consolidation of purpose in the community, is no longer needed, there has been some disintegration of communal organizations.

Particularly, where there has been intermarriage with whites, a note of individualism has crept into some sections, and the sharing of one's possessions is no longer regarded as obligatory. Such a practice is condemned by the Indian group, which manifests its disapproval by ostracism of the ones in disrepute. This has resulted in conflicts and confusion in the communities. The mixed bloods fluctuate between the patterns of the Indians and those of the whites, and hence the full acceptance by either group is denied them.

Where the segregation from whites is more marked, individualism is less apparent, and social pressure by the group is still more intense. Among the Hopis of Arizona, living in a closely knit society bounded by ties of kinship, marriage, and race, it is a matter of grave consequence for a member to break the prevailing order. It is impossible for him to live down the mistakes in the eyes of his fellow men, and a broken promise is never forgotten. That his infractions are continually talked about and his shame pointed out, have been known to drive some violators insane.

And so it is with many forms of their ancient culture. In whole or in part, the Indian has clung to the customs of his ancestors. No matter what we find Indians doing today, whether they are

Following the ancient custom of her people, she pounds the acorns in a stone hole with a stone pestle until they are ground into meal.

FRESNO COUNTY, CALIFORNIA

working in an airplane factory for white men, driving white men's tractors across their fields, or attending white men's schools, once back among their own people they take part in the ceremonies, the dances, and tribal customs as before.

But following the customs of their ancestors no longer brings the official disapproval upon the Indians it once did. Their habits, beliefs, and crafts are no longer frowned upon or forbidden by the Government because they are not like those of white men. Instead, the white men are at last recognizing the right of Indian culture to survive and the right of the Indian to live his own life in his own way just as we desire to live our lives in our own way.

The ground acorn meal is thoroughly sifted. Mixed with water, it will soon become acorn mush, a favorite Indian dish.

FRESNO COUNTY, CALIFORNIA

Adobe ovens are used by Pueblo women for baking bread. On the metate (the stone slab at the left of the oven), corn is ground into meal.

SAN JUAN PUEBLO, NEW MEXICO

Pima Indians make large storage baskets of straw, twigs, and adobe. This one is about four feet in diameter. Placed on supports to keep them from the damp ground, the grain is stored in them. Tin covers are usually placed on top.

SALT RIVER INDIAN RESERVATION, ARIZONA

An Arapaho cleans out the fire pit of a smoke house. This frame will be covered with brush, and meat will be hung inside to smoke.

CHEYENNE RESERVATION, OKLAHOMA

A Pomo woman with her primitive drill bores a hole in a piece of clamshell.
Once used for wampum the beads she now makes will be strung for ornaments.

PINOLEVILLE, CALIFORNIA

Tattooing, a custom once widely practiced, still prevails among some tribes today. This Apache woman wears a blue mark between her eyes and numerous designs on her forearm.

FORT McDOWELL, ARIZONA

7. *Religion*

THE clouds hung dark and heavy over the ancient pueblo of San Ildefonso near the banks of the Rio Grande. The plaza lay strangely quiet and expectant in the warm spring air, and little life moved about the terraced houses. From somewhere underneath the ground came a pulsing, rhythmic sound that grew louder and louder and then almost imperceptibly dimmed into silence, leaving among its hearers a sensation of eeriness and mystery, and the doubt as to whether the sound had really existed. Again the steady beat was felt and heard, for these were reverberations from the tomtoms in the kiva below, where the men were preparing for a tribal dance. Suddenly the plaza was no longer quiet. From the ladder of the kiva, there emerged strange-looking men with feathers and pieces of cotton stuck in their long, black hair. Their faces and bodies were painted dark red, and from their shoulders hung brown and white deer skins. Around their ankles were tiny bells which made music as they walked, and in one hand was held a bow and in the other a gourd which rattled in time to their movements.

About to be performed was one of their seasonal dances—a dance shrouded in aboriginal mysticism—known as the Bow and Arrow

Dance. Facing north, the men formed a straight line, and the dance was begun. It consisted principally of a forceful stamping of the feet in rhythmic beats with vigorous movements of the arms. Accompanying these rhythmic motions was a chant, sung by the dancers and emphasized at appropriate intervals by the rattle of gourds. The dance continued without much noticeable change for about a half hour, and then quietly the men climbed the steps of the kiva and disappeared down the ladder.

From the doors of the adobe houses around the plaza, came women bearing trays of food, which they carried to the steps of the kiva to be received by the men. The women were not allowed to enter this sacred chamber and so retired to their homes. When the meal had been consumed, the dancers once again returned to the plaza, and this time they faced south.[1] All day long this procedure continued, now facing west, now facing east—the same dance, the same chant, and the steady beat of tomtoms underground.

What had been our opportunity to witness was one of the religious rituals of the American Indian. It was his way of invoking his god for the blessing he most needed.

In order to comprehend the significance of the Indian religious ceremony it is necessary to understand the religious concepts of the Indian and how they developed.

Thousands of years ago the native aboriginal feared the winds that destroyed his home, the storms and wild beasts that brought harm to his crops. He was fearful of the great rocks which could

[1] This dance, as in most Indian dances, was directed toward the home of the four winds.

82

This California Indian roundhouse, once the scene of many happy tribal gatherings and ceremonies, is seldom used today. There are few ceremonial houses left in California today due to long contact with whites and the resultant weakening of Indian religion.

MENDOCINO COUNTY, CALIFORNIA

crush him or the rushing waters that might carry him out to sea. These things he could not fight with a bow and arrow, and so like a child he asked help from the Great Mother Nature. He felt that the clouds, the night, the moon, even the trees possessed immortal life and that by appealing to them they would bring him good fortune and success. In order, therefore, to invoke the blessing and protection of these unseen powers or gods, the Indian performed sacrifices, dances, and chants. He developed strange syllables and luck charms and songs and ceremonies that might cajole or coerce the spirits into granting him power and security. In all this he believed and had faith and so created a religion.

For generations the Indians have clung to their beliefs in spite of all the forces that have tried to change them—powerful forces exerted toward this end. For after the white settlers came, missionaries from Catholic and Protestant churches went forth to convert these "heathens" and to save their souls; and the many ramifications of Christian practices were spread over a race of people whose gods were pagan. The American Government, established by a people who came to these shores in search of this same religious freedom, officially frowned upon any manifestation of native belief. It was a form of barbarism to be discouraged and extinguished. When it placed the Indians under its jurisdiction, the abrogation of their constitutional rights, particularly in regard to religion, was put into effect. Children enrolled in the governmental schools were forbidden to practice their own religion and were forced to join a Christian sect. They were to attend the church of that sect and receive instructions in its precepts. All ceremonies on many reservations, no matter how harmless, were

Kivas are found in all Pueblos. These are underground chambers, reached by a ladder from the roof, where religious ceremonials and rituals are held. Only on special occasions are Indian women allowed to enter them.

SAN ILDEFONSO, NEW MEXICO

prohibited, and force was employed in many instances to make the men cut their hair short—a tribal and religious affront. But they were dealing with a people whose rites and beliefs had persisted for centuries, and whose faith was imperishable. They might seem to do as the white man dictated, but underneath lingered the strange potency of their own beliefs, and, when it was possible, they continued their practices in secret. In 1934 the Government finally issued an order which prohibited any interference with Indian religious life in accordance with one of the first principles of our Constitution. Now they are free to have their own rituals and ceremonies or to follow any faith they desire. Many Indians have joined Protestant or Catholic churches and some, while belonging to the Christian church, continue to participate in the religious rites and ceremonies of their own tribes.

An important adjunct of Indian rites and ceremonies is the dance. This in itself is an art and demands many years of careful training. While some dances are purely social and many others, from which most of the sacred or religious parts have been removed, are performed at carnivals or fairs attended by the public, the real religious dances of the Indian are very significant and sacred occasions possessing great dignity and beauty. These are held at certain seasons of the year in connection with the planting or harvesting of the corn or the killing of game in the hunting season. There are dances invoking the gods for rain, and there are dances for gratitude or mourning.

The steps, music, costumes, and purpose of the dances vary according to the tribes. For example: The Hopi Indians perform a Kachina Dance and wear weird-looking masks to represent the

The Kachina cult is one of the dominant religious cults of the Pueblo Indians. The kachinas, or mythical beings, are believed to visit the villages on particular occasions, at which time they are impersonated by Indian dancers. At these ceremonies small cottonwood images of kachina dancers are made by the men as presents for little girls. Playing with these dolls, the young become familiar with the complicated masks and costumes worn during religious festivals. The doll shown above represents one of many kachina dancers.

Kachinas, who are supernatural beings in which the tribe believes. There is the Fire Ceremony of the Navajo, the intricate and graceful Eagle Dance of the Pueblo Tewa, the elaborate Buffalo Dance of the Sioux, and the Green Corn Dance of the Creek. There are many more, all of them colorful and dramatic, especially when accompanied by the beating of the tomtoms, or chants and singing.

Other demonstrations of their beliefs are held in secret. For this purpose there is often a specially constructed ceremonial house. In the kiva of the Pueblo, the medicine hogan of the Navajo, and certain tipis or lodges of other tribes, sacred rites are performed. These rites are of such importance to the Indians and guarded so carefully that few white men have had the privilege of attending them.

Symbolic objects are often used in connection with the ceremonies, such as fetishes, prayer sticks, or "sacred bundles" which may contain a pipe, arrows, tobacco, or whatever has a peculiar significance to the tribe's ritual.

Indians believe also in the existence of the soul after death. For them a man continues to live in another land following the same occupation as he had when he was alive. Because of this belief there are men and women in every tribe who are supposed to have power to call back the spirits of the dead to talk with living relatives.

In all the life about him, then, there exists for the Indian, powers which are animate and must be respected. Even during social celebrations certain religious customs are observed. For example: Every year in Nevada, during the week of the Fourth of July,

88

Masks are worn by the Hopi Indians during their Kachina dances. The one above represents one of the supernatural beings in which the tribe believes.

PHOTOGRAPHED THROUGH THE COURTESY OF THE LABO-RATORY OF ANTHROPOLOGY AT SANTA FE, NEW MEXICO

the Western Paiute and Shoshoni pack their families and baggage in wagons and travel to a particular spot along the river bottom at Owyhee. Here they make camp, being very careful to arrange the tipis in a semicircle with the opening to the east. This is to permit the sun, their ancient creator, to enter the camp each morning and watch over them during the day. The days are spent in the activities of a rodeo, and during the evenings the same recreations enjoyed by their forefathers are engaged in. The old people sit in groups and play the ancient stick game [2] while the younger ones perform the old tribal dances accompanied by the rhythm of the drums.

One could go on indefinitely describing the beliefs and rituals of the various 200 tribes that live in America, their intense conservatism, their reverence for the past and the world of nature about them; but in a brief documentary treatment of this kind it is impossible. It is enough that we understand what a powerful force religion is in their everyday life, their politics, their economic and social life, and even in their games. For to understand this is to understand to a small degree the outrage felt by a people, who until a few short years ago were forbidden religious freedom.

If the performance of ceremonies or the wearing of amulets produce a calm comfort and the feeling of a power greater than the individual, which offers hope and security—the essence of religion is present, and under any other name is the same the world over. Even if the rites and beliefs of Indian religion differ from ours, even if his faith in the power of magic or of the spirits provokes

[2] A number of sticks are shuffled and divided. One of the sticks is oddly marked, and the object of the game is to guess in which heap the odd stick is concealed.

Indians are free to follow any religious faith they desire. Though many tribes continue to practice their own religion, some Indians have become members of the Christian faith. In this Indian pueblo is a Catholic church, one of many established in the Southwest, where the Spanish and members of the Franciscan order attempted to convert the Indians as early as 1542.

TESUQUE PUEBLO, NEW MEXICO

incredulousness, it must be remembered that there is no historical religion in the world without its adulterations of magic. There survive in them all the relics of coercive rites and persuasive supplications, not unlike those of the Indians. The demonstrations, the belief that a bone of a saint will cure a particular malady, the belief that a certain formula is indispensable to the efficacy of a prayer—these things are relics of magic rites. Only a rare few have been able to find religion in abstract ideas naked of ceremonial adornment. For the rest—the pageantry of a high mass in the Notre Dame Cathedral, the simplicity of a "Meeting" in a New England village church, or the beat of the tomtoms in an Indian Pueblo—faith is there, and so, too, religion.

8. *Disease and Health*

DISEASE flourishes when people live in cramped, badly ventilated houses, when they have no means of proper sewage or garbage disposal, and when their water supply is limited or contaminated. Disease flourishes when people are undernourished from lack of fresh fruits, vegetables, and milk and when they have not enough clothes to keep them warm. It spreads rapidly among those who do not know the ordinary rules of sanitation and hygiene and who are ignorant as to the care and segregation of the sick. Poor housing and lack of money has placed the majority of Indians in that group known as the "ill-housed, ill-fed, and ill-clothed." Good health cannot be maintained under these conditions, and disease is difficult to control.

Some of the diseases found to be most prevalent among the Indians are tuberculosis, pneumonia, and trachoma (an eye infection leading to blindness). Other diseases like measles, mumps, chicken pox, and whooping cough often develop into serious and fatal epidemics. This is partly due to the fact that the Indian seems to have less resistance to the white man's diseases and partly because the proper treatment is not understood. Tuberculosis was present among Indians before the arrival of the white men, but it has

93

increased to tremendous proportions since the Indians no longer live the rugged outdoor life they were once accustomed to. It has become, therefore, one of the most dangerous threats to Indian life. In Alaska, where diet and living conditions are exceptionally poor, the native death rate from tuberculosis alone is approximately thirteen times that of the United States altogether.

In the days prior to white men and white doctors, Indian ills were treated by professional "healers," of whom a large number existed. They were known as medicine men, and their art was rooted in sorcery. Today they are still present among many tribes carrying on their practices in the same manner as those before them. The medicine man is supposed to be endowed with a special knowledge and power over the potent and unseen forces or demons that cause disease. When he is called in for the sick, he usually inquires of his patient what he has done to offend the evil powers. The patient tells him of a bad dream or some religious rule he has broken which he thinks has angered the spirits and brought about this punishment. Accordingly, the shaman selects a particular treatment and ceremony for the sick person. He may prescribe a mixture of herbs, a massage, or a sweat bath. Then he usually sings a chant and performs a special dance to drive the evil spirits from the victim's body. Charms, snakes, or sand paintings are often employed to assist him in effecting a cure. Such a method of treating the sick may seem very strange to us, but it is interesting to know that these "curing ceremonies" are not forbidden by the Government today. This is mainly because they are so closely connected with Indian religion. Also, it is realized that the faith of a sick Indian in the song-prayers and accom-

"Squatters' Village" on a dump outside of Carson City, Nevada, where non-ward Indians live. Surroundings such as these make disease an ever-present danger.

panying ceremony often contributes to his recovery. The herbs used by the medicine men contain certain drugs which are found in our medical prescriptions today, such as cascara, ipecac, and cocaine, and even massages and sweat baths are part of modern treatment for specific ills. We find, therefore, that the Indians who have been "cured" regard the medicine man as having some special powers; and his influence, particularly on the full-blood Indian, is still impressive.

Because of this, as well as the fact that for generations Indians knew nothing of modern medicine or hygiene, it has not been a simple matter to teach them about disease prevention and control. The doctor or dentist, with his shiny sharp instruments, his X-ray machines and bottles of medicine, is often regarded with fear or suspicion by the Indian who has been used to ceremonies and magic charms. It has been difficult to persuade him that a hospital with its clean white operating rooms and strange smell of disinfectant is far better for a serious illness than the dark, crowded room of his wigwam or hogan.[1] To educate him in the value of scientific medical treatment has been a slow process, for health education on a large scale was not attempted until 1924, when it became an important activity of the United States Indian Service.

Since then the pressing needs of health control have been met in part by federal and state health departments and by some of the schools as well. Medical clinics have been established on many reservations or in towns where Indians can go for aid and advice. Eighty hospitals and fourteen tuberculosis sanatoria have been

[1] Indians believed that no one should live in a house where there has been a death. This belief, still quite prevalent, presented an additional hurdle in overcoming the fear of hospitalization.

96

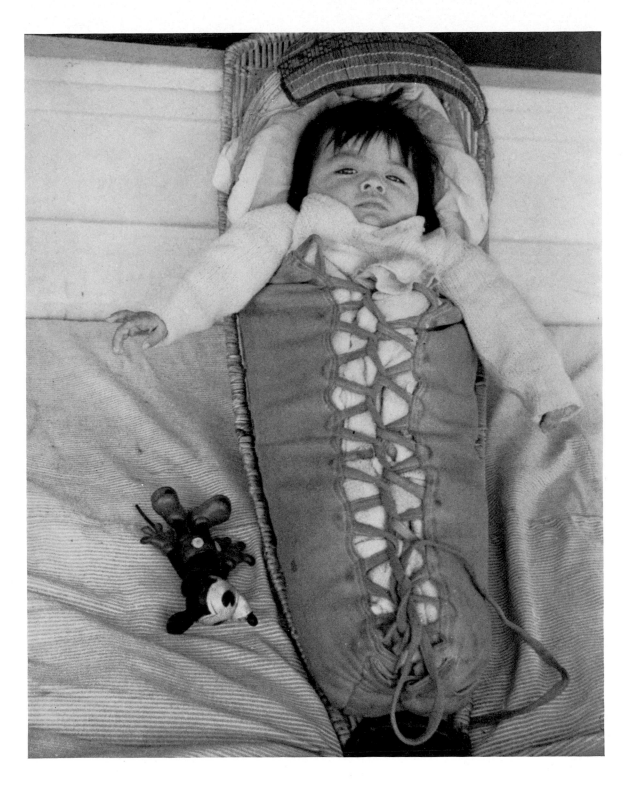

A papoose, with his Mickey Mouse, recovers from an illness on the porch of a Government Hospital. Because he is more accustomed to his cradle board than a hospital bed, he is allowed to remain in it for a limited time.

CARSON INDIAN AGENCY, NEVADA

built to care for the sick and to prevent contagion. In 1939, 55,460 Indians were treated in them. Indian mothers are beginning to see the advantages of sanitation and medical aid when their children are born, and many lives have consequently been saved by hospitalization. Specially equipped automobiles with operating tables or dental chairs are driven by doctors to far distant points to examine Indians, vaccinate them, set broken bones, or give medical aid they would otherwise lack. Public health nurses visit the homes, and lectures are given to mothers in the care of their children or in the importance and technique of treating minor illnesses.

In many day schools, well-balanced noon meals are served to provide ill-nourished bodies with necessary vitamins. The importance of cleanliness is stressed, and many day schools provide showers and laundries for the children and parents of the community.

A great hazard to Indian health is the number of dilapidated and unsanitary privies so frequently found in Indian communities. There is usually only one to a number of families, and the flimsy construction makes them a natural breeding ground for germs. Where there have been available funds to do so, the Government has replaced these with well-screened and ventilated ones, thereby helping to reduce the spread of typhoid and dysentery.

There is yet much to be accomplished in the field of Indian health before any great degree of improvement is attained. While the Indian death rate has decreased considerably in recent years, it is still much higher than that of the white population. However, the education of the Indian youth today will undoubtedly result

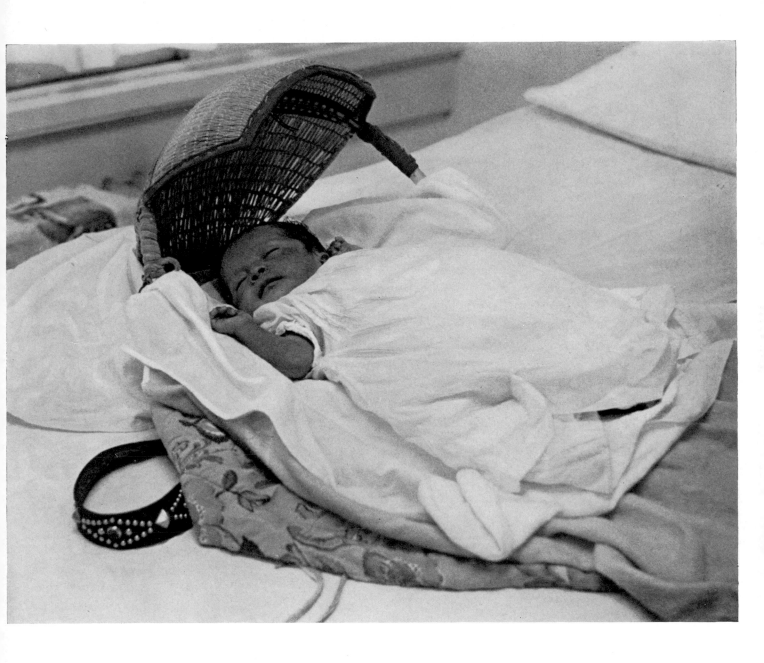

The great majority of Indian mothers now have their babies in hospitals. But the acceptance of modern obstetrics does not necessarily indicate the repudiation of other Indian customs. Hence, this Washo infant is placed in his primitive cradle, following the ancient practice.

CARSON AGENCY HOSPITAL, NEVADA

in improved methods of living and consequently in stronger bodies. Sick Indians cannot be expected to work efficiently or improve their surroundings. Their health must be restored and with it their old tribal reputation of strength.

This man's blindness was probably caused by trachoma, a dread scourge to the Indian race. With the recent discovery of the effectiveness of sulfanilamide treatments, this disease has been greatly checked by the Indian Service Health Division.

SAN ILDEFONSO, NEW MEXICO

Breeders of disease are the two Indian privies shown above. Left, a sanitary privy built by the Government is well constructed and ventilated and will prevent flies from carrying dangerous germs.

Upper left. OUTSIDE CARSON CITY, NEVADA

Upper right. DRESSLERVILLE, NEVADA

Left. FRESNO CO., CALIFORNIA

9. *Education*

THE future of the Indians, as the future of all peoples, depends upon its youth. How well-fitted Indian youth will be for the life they will lead among white men as well as among their own people depends largely upon their education.

The American aboriginals had their own system of education. The children's schools were their homes and the world of land and sky. Their instructors were their parents, grandparents, and the elements of nature from which they learned many things pertinent to the life they were to lead. Little children played at the serious business of adult life. From their earliest days the closest association between parents and children existed in matters of education. Constant admonition, praise, or disparagement were the mediums used by the parents in training and disciplining the children. They were furnished with appropriate toys or miniature objects of those articles made or used by their parents in everyday life. They became amateur potters, basketmakers, or weavers. They learned to cook, to be expert with the bow, to attend the crops: the girls following the pursuits of their mothers and the boys those of their fathers. Their laws, customs, tribal beliefs, and myths, all things within the range of instruction limited only by their pertinence to the tribe, were subjects communicated to the young.

From living close to the land and depending on it for their lives, the children observed closely the behavior of the wild life about them and the changing moods of the skies, the forests, and waters. From these they learned by trial and error what was to be feared and what was friendly. By seeing and doing, therefore, and by unconscious absorption, the Indian child finally grew into the accomplished man or woman whose eyes and ears were keen and whose hands were efficient.

With the arrival of the white man and his rapid domination of Indian life, native educational methods were revolutionized, and the effect, designed or undesigned, was a profound one. All whites became instructors and all Indians, young or old, became pupils; and the Indian passed at once into the iron age of his development. His native ways were discouraged. The deliberate breakup of his tribal and family life was sought and gained, and the dominant motives behind the educational programs forced on him were those which would make him live as the white man and become "civilized." These efforts were in part realized in the form of boarding schools in which children, torn from their parents, were placed. In these, they were made to endure militaristic regimes, inadequate food, overwork, inferior staffs, and genuine cruelty—a concentration camp as the price of having been born an Indian.

When a number of years had passed, the children were allowed to return to their homes. Now it was difficult to get used to the primitive way of living again. Sleeping on earth floors, the food,

A little Navajo boy, who does not yet go to school, spends the long days alone watching his mother's sheep. Only at dusk does he return to his hogan.

NAVAJO RESERVATION, NEW MEXICO

the ceremonies, and even the language of their parents and friends were hard to become accustomed to once more. The things they had been taught at school were of little value for the life they were to lead on the reservation. The old people disapproved of the white customs their children had acquired, and the young educated Indian was now more unhappy and maladjusted than ever.

By 1929 the evils of this educational program, long recognized by friends of the Indians, were terminated by the creation of a new educational policy. Many boarding schools were closed or reduced in size, and day schools were built on the reservations to enable children to go to school and yet live at home. There are now three hundred and fifty of these schools besides the many public schools, attended voluntarily by Indian children. The parents are pleased with the schools today and encourage their children to go to them. In ten years the Indian day school population increased from 4,532 to 14,087, and today attendance in all the schools is 73,709.

However, the building of more schools or the enrollment of more children does not solve all the problems present today in the field of Indian education. It must be recalled here, that these school children represent more than three hundred different tribes and fifty-five linguistic groups—two hundred and fifty if we consider dialectical differences. The English language—and some Spanish in the Southwest—is the only common one of communication, and this is not universal. About 50,000 Indians speak neither language, and illiteracy is estimated at about 30%. The difficulties to be overcome in this one aspect alone are particularly emphasized

No longer separated by force from their parents and sent off to non-reservation boarding schools, young Navajo children now attend one of the modern day schools on their own reservation. Here they learn to speak English, a language only 10% of their tribe can understand.

FORT DEFIANCE, ARIZONA

in the case of the Navajo, where approximately 90% of the people neither speak nor understand English.

Indian boarding and day schools under the jurisdiction of the present Department of Indian Affairs are now striving to fit the Indian child for the life he will follow as an Indian. Vocational emphasis in education is increasing and instruction in farming, mechanics, building, the care and raising of livestock, the conservation of land, etc., are a few of the necessary subjects now included in such programs. Girls are given instruction in domestic science as well as other pertinent courses, with the aim of fitting them into the pattern of their probable future life.

Other subjects which are becoming increasingly important are those concerned with the arts and crafts. Indians are born artists, and in the past they have contributed much to American art. Some tribes were extremely skilled in the art of weaving fine blankets, those of the Navajo being most famous. The silver and turquoise jewelry of the Navajo and Zuni, the graceful pottery of the Pueblo, and the baskets of the Apache, Pima, and Pomo (whose baskets are considered by some to be the finest in the world) are works of art to be found in prized museum collections. The imaginative and symbolic decorations that were painted on the tipis of the Plains Indians and the exquisite and highly conventionalized sand paintings of the Navajo are beautiful examples of design, color, and detail. Because the artistic value of their work was appreciated by few people, Indian art degenerated into cheap, easily manufactured articles to satisfy the demands of the majority who wanted Indian curios and trinkets. Real Indian art, therefore, has rapidly deteriorated.

This schoolroom of Washo Indian children looks much like any other schoolroom in America. Coming from near-by communities, these youngsters, like white children, learn arithmetic, reading, music, and drawing. Many Indian children attend public schools.

DRESSLERVILLE, NEVADA

To prevent this obvious loss to America, a governmental Arts and Crafts Board was formed to encourage and stimulate Indian art. In the schools, courses have been introduced in which older tribal artists are the instructors. The girls are taught intricate bead work, and to make baskets, pottery, and blankets of fine design and texture. The boys learn the crafts of their forefathers and how the Navajo and Zuni made their elaborate silver bridles, necklaces, and bracelets. They melt the silver, mold and design it into individual and attractive patterns, and take great pride in their creations.

Painting, too, once confined to the decoration of skins or bark, has become particularly popular, especially among Pueblo boys. Many have been found to have exceptional talent for line, rhythm, and color, and some of their water colors and murals have won national recognition.

Learning in the schools to produce real works of art will not only keep a valuable native art alive in America, but it will provide the Indian with an avocation from which he may reap pecuniary benefits.

But vocational and avocational emphasis alone is not enough. Due regard must be given to the varied needs of the different tribal and sectional groups.

The variety of cultures represented by the many groups of children obviously demands the intelligent formulation of an educational program recognizing these differences and prepared to deal with them. There are children who come from a Pueblo culture or the seminomadic one of the Navajo. There are the Cherokee from the woodland area, the Pima group, who are

These young boys receive instruction in farming at this Indian day school. When they grow older, they will be able to raise good crops and help support their families.

PINOLEVILLE, CALIFORNIA

essentially a farming people, the cattle-raising Papago from an arid region, the Kiowa from the plains, and the Hopi, who live in villages. These are not all, but they represent diverse social groups which cannot be merged into one homogeneous unit and approached as such by educators. The more astute members of the Division of Education in the Indian Service are striving to remedy this situation, but in spite of their efforts a travesty is still being made of the word education in so far as it may be defined as preparing a child for his future life. It would seem obvious that anyone connected with the education of Indians would be fairly cognizant of these distinct requirements and would, therefore, adapt to them the curricula and instruction most fitting. Yet with a few outstanding exceptions this is not so. In the public schools, of course, it is impossible to adjust entire programs to the needs of a few Indian children, but in schools where the enrollment is predominantly or wholly Indian, teachers should prepare the students for the life they will lead on their reservation or in their community. Instruction in cattle raising will be of little value to a group whose land is overgrazed and scarred by great washes and which will grow nothing but sagebrush and cactus. The vital need here is apparent. The study of soil, the prevention of erosion and proper cultivation is clearly indicated. Instruction in plumbing and electric wiring to a group who will return to a reservation where work of this kind is nonavailable is hardly compatible with common sense.

To provide these children with a knowledge they can take back to their reservations, which can be used to improve conditions on the reservations and enable them to make a decent living, will

At the Phoenix Indian School, advanced students receive training in tractor and Diesel motor operations. This school, drawing Indian students from many reservations in the state, recognizes tribal differences and divides its primary classes according to tribes. Each group is instructed in the social and economic problems of its own reservation.

PHOENIX, ARIZONA

be a definite contribution toward the rehabilitation of their lives.

Assimilation presents an additional problem in education. Where it exists, the adjustment of the Indian to the white varies greatly and is nowhere complete. In the public schools more and more Indian children are being enrolled, particularly in Minnesota, California, and Washington, where assimilation of the Indians is proceeding rapidly. (Payment for these services is made by the Federal Government.) But comprehension of the complexities in adjustment for the Indians is sorely lacking on the part of most schools.

For the child who comes from a social environment so radically different from that of the white child, whose life is almost completely tied to the land, whose relationships to the state and national governments differ from the whites, and who in all probability will return to his reservation or community, the prevailing academic program found in most public schools is inadequate to meet his practical needs. In many of these schools, teachers complain that Indian children do not grasp ideas as fast as the white children but report that they excel in work which they do with their hands, particularly drawing. That the younger Indian child finds it difficult to compete with the whites, considering in the majority of cases his English or understanding of it is limited, that he is coping for the first time with an entirely new set of ideas, that his anomalous position is not made easy by the frequent insinuations of most white children that he is dirty and diseased or an inferior type of being, and that in too many instances his teachers have no understanding or knowledge themselves of Indian

At the Phoenix Indian school a Navajo and a Pima boy help to harvest the large crop of spinach they and other students have raised. The spinach will be canned by the girls and used at the school. What is left over will be traded with other Indian schools for their surplus produce.

PHOENIX INDIAN SCHOOL, PHOENIX, ARIZONA

children and their problems, is not to be wondered at in the light of these facts, nor is it surprising that he often leaves school at an early age and prefers to remain at home.

It is not a simple task to make the adjustment of Indian life with that of the white in one generation or two; but the adoption of a curriculum which will fit the practical requirements of rural and agricultural life, the selection of teachers for schools containing a reasonable number of Indian children, who can fill the necessary requirements called forth by the presence of Indians, would be a step in relieving a situation fraught with problems.

The tactics used in the past, in which everything possible was done to turn Indian children away from all things Indian and to draw them into a new kind of civilization which was in so many ways alien to their own philosophy of life, drove them back to their reservations confused, discontented, and bitter. These devices, it is to be hoped, are definitely of the past. The Indian must be helped now to help himself, and herein lies the fundamental objective in the education of Indian children.

Such expert basketmakers as this Pomo woman are rapidly disappearing. To revive the Indian arts and crafts, Indian schools are now providing courses in them.

HOPLAND, CALIFORNIA

An old Maricopa woman polishes her sun-baked pottery with a stone. Indian schools are now employing such tribal artists to teach the children these ancient crafts.

LEHI, ARIZONA

A young Indian painter at the Santa Fe Indian School. Many Indians have remarkable talent for painting, and some of their work has won national recognition.

SANTA FE, NEW MEXICO

A Navajo boy learns the silver craftsmanship for which his people are so famous. Here he works on a beautiful silver bridle.

SANTA FE INDIAN SCHOOL, SANTA FE, NEW MEXICO

Summary

The contributions to American life by the Indians have been numerous. Some of these have played a large part in the commerce of the world, such as tobacco, cocoa, cotton, and rubber. The Indians passed on to the white man many valuable foods including corn, squash, beans, tomatoes, pumpkins, peanuts, and maple sugar. Many drugs we now find to be indispensable were discovered by them, for instance quinine, witch hazel, ipecac, and cocaine. They contributed also to a number of sports we enjoy today: canoeing, snowshoeing, tobogganing, lacrosse, and archery. They have enriched our lives by their talent for making beautiful baskets, blankets, paintings, jewelry, and pottery; and their colorful songs and dances have given America a folklore distinctly its own.

For all these gifts and many more we are indebted to the Indian, but for a time America seemed to forget this. Treaties were broken regardless of our national honor. The Indian was thrust aside, for, according to our standards, he seemed backward and inferior. His intelligence was doubted, and we were prejudiced because his color was different from ours. He could not become a white man, and yet we tried to destroy his Indian way of life.

But today much of this has changed. The Indian now has hope; for the white man is beginning not only to aid him but to understand him. He has at last been recognized as an inventive and intelligent being whose poverty is not entirely the result of his own doing, who, while his opportunities have been less than ours, is neither superior nor inferior to other peoples. His talents and abilities are being looked upon with respect. Even his way of living, his helping and working with his fellow man, his contentment with a life of simplicity, his love of beauty, his dignity and courtesy, his respect for nature and leisure, are beginning to be valued in a world harassed by those elements which are in direct contrast to such a way of life.

Given the opportunity to raise his standard of living and to regain his national pride, the Indian will not only enrich his own life but that of America as well.

The young have a new hope.

Bibliography

COOLIDGE, M. R. and D., *The Navajo Indians*. Cambridge, Mass.: Houghton Mifflin Co., 1930.

DIXON, R. B., *The Racial History of Mankind*. New York: Charles Scribner's Sons, 1923.

EMBREE, E., *Indians of the Americas*. Cambridge, Mass.: Houghton Mifflin Co., 1939.

FRAZER, SIR J., *The Golden Bough*. New York: The Macmillan Co., 1900.

JENNINGS, C. W., *The Red Men and the New World Drama*. Washington, D. C.: Press of W. L. Roberts Co.

KIDDER, A. V., *An Introduction to the Study of Southwestern Archaeology with a Preliminary Account of the Excavations at Pecos*. New Haven: Yale Press, 1924.

KROEBER, A. L., *Anthropology*. New York: Harcourt Brace & Co., 1923.

LOWIE, R. H., *Primitive Religion*. New York: Boni & Liveright, 1924.

PARSONS, E. C., *Pueblo Indian Religion*. Chicago: University of Chicago Press, 1939. Vol. II.

RADIN, P., *Story of the American Indian*. New York: Horace Liveright, Inc., 1927.

SCHMECKEBIER, L. F., *The Office of Indian Affairs*. Institute for Government Research No. 48. Baltimore: The Johns Hopkins Press, 1927.

Smithsonian Institution, Bureau of American Ethnology. Bulletin 30, *Handbook of American Indians*. 4th impression. Washington, D. C.: U. S. Gov. Printing Office, 1912.

Smithsonian Scientific Series. *The North American Indians*. Compiled by R. A. Palmer. New York: Smithsonian Institution Series, Inc., 1929, 1934.

VAILLANT, G. C., *Indian Arts in North America*. New York: Harper & Bros., 1939.

WISSLER, C., *The American Indian*. 3rd edition. New York: Oxford University Press, 1938.

WISSLER, C., *Indians of the United States*. New York: Doubleday, Doran & Co., 1940.

Bulletins

COLLIER, J., Office of Indian Affairs. Reprinted from the Annual Report of the Secretary of the Interior, Washington, D. C., 1938.

COLLIER, J., Reprint of Talk Given at Bacone College, Muskogee, Oklahoma, 1937. #132830, Washington, D. C.

Indians At Work. U. S. Dept. of the Interior, Sept., 1938; Jan., July, Dec., 1939; Jan., April, 1940.

A New Day for the Indians. New York: Academy Press, 1938.

Human Dependency and Economic Survey. Sacramento Indian Jurisdiction, California. Issued jointly by the Office of Indian Affairs, Dept. of the Interior, and Technical Cooperation, Bureau of Indian Affairs—Soil Conservation Dept., Dept. of Agriculture, Washington, D. C.

A Brief Statement on the Background of Present-Day Indian Policy in the United States. U. S. Dept. of the Interior, 1938. #45526, Washington, D. C.

Indians and the Land. Contributions by the Delegation of the U. S. First Inter-American Conference on Indian Life. Pátzcuaro, Mexico, 1940, Washington, D. C.

The Legal Status of the Indians in the United States. Felix Cohen. U. S. Dept. of the Interior, 1940. #96571-B, Washington, D. C.

Indian Education. Division of Education, Dept. of the Interior. #31, 1939, and #42 & 44, 1940. Washington, D. C.

Introduction to American Indian Art. Parts 1 and 2. Exposition of Indian Tribal Arts, Inc. Sloan, J., and La Farge, O., New York, 1931.

Makah
Ozette
Quileute
Hoh
Quinaielt
Skokomish
Galice Creek,
Rogue River,
Meguenodon,
Clackamas,
Calapooya,
Umpqua,
Klamath,
Tututni,
& Shasta

Lummi
Swinomish
Tulalip
Muckleshoot
Nisqually
Chehalis
Yakima

Colville Kalispel
Spokane
WASH
Coeur d'Alene
Umatilla,
Cayuse & Walla Walla
Nez Percé

Blackfeet

Sioux &
Assiniboine
Chippewa
& Cree
Gros Ventre
& Assiniboine

Chippewa

Arikara,
Mandan,
& Gros Ventre

N.D.

Paiute,
Tenino & Wasco
ORE
Klamath &
Modoc

MONT

Crow
Cheyenne
Sioux
Sioux

29
24

IDAHO
Shoshone

18

19

Arapaho &
Shoshone

15

12 S.D.
Sio

16

Hoopa &
Klamath

Pit River
Paiute

Paiute &
Shoshone
20
Bannock

WYO

Sioux

Paiute
25

CAL

26

Paiute

NEV

Goshute

Goshute

UTAH

Ute

21

COLO

NEB

Po

Pot

KAN

Po
Paw
Tonka
Otoe & K

Paiutes

Paiute

Shivwits

Ute
Paiute
Kaibab

Tule
River

Inyo

Paiute

Havasupai

Walapi
27

NAVAJO
HOPI
22

Apache

Kickapoo & Iowa

Cheyenne & Arapaho

See

Mission Indians

Mojave

Chemehuevi &
Mojave

ARIZ
Pima

Zuni
Pueblo

Apache
28

N.M.

Caddo,
Delaware,
Wichita,
Kiowa,
Comanche,
& Apache

Yuma
Gila

Cocopah

Apache

23
Apache

TEXAS

Papago

Maricopa

Marks thus + re-
present small
Indian communities
called "Rancherias"
in California, and
"Colonies" in Nevada.

MEXICO

Other Reservations are named after the Tribes living on them.